Poem a Day
May
2018

Cat and Cyro Hartliebe

With exclusive poems by
Skyling De'Ambroise
Moe Destoryer
and Beulah Pockets

DEDICATION

To everyone
Especially Grandma

Family and Friends

I am the Youngest in the House
Cyro Hartliebe

I am the youngest in the house.
I am not alone.
There are five others with me.

The oldest is Pop Pop.
He buys me things.

Grandma is next.
She lets me play on her phone.

Third is Uncle Dave.
He takes me to Tae Kwon Do.

Uncle Bill is fourth.
He plays games with me.

Last is Mommy.
She teaches me stuff.

I am the youngest in the house.
I love being me.

Thank You

Moe Destoryer

To the one that raised you

To the one that protected you

To the one who taught you

To the one who is most important to you

To all the mothers I know

Thank you

Breakfast in Bed
Cat Hartliebe

The roasted bean ground down to nothing
Cooked in steaming water
Placed in a cup with milk or cream

Move to a tray with breakfast wonder
Eggs and toast and juice
Head to the farthest bedroom

Lying in the bed still asleep
Wake up with the smell of coffee
"Happy Mother's Day!"

Maps and Mom
Beulah Pockets

We all have our passions

The things we love most

It might be books or fashion

Eating food or chasing ghosts

But of all the affections

That someone could have

My mother's most favorite

Is talking directions

Give her a map and give her joy

She thinks it not at all odd

That the map of Atlantic Canada

Is her most beloved toy

It may seem weird

That she thinks routes have zing

But hey, whatever

We all have our thing

Not Alone
Cat Hartliebe

The unwelcoming feeling

Of sitting alone in absence.

Nothing's around.

Or is it that you just cannot see?

The enveloping sensation

Of wondering if things are here.

Something's around...

Isn't it? What is that sound?

The welcoming touch

Of someone you love.

Someone's around.

Sight isn't needed to feel calm.

Mother Store
Cat Hartliebe

Some days I wish I could go to the Mother Store
It would be down on the corner
Passed the library and marketplace
Where everyone can find the perfect mom
The store that has every type of mother

The mothers who cuddle under blankets on a cold wet night
The mothers who bake cookies and cake on the weekend
The mothers who can fix broken arms and calm boo boos
The mothers who read every night and morning
Even if the story is the exact same one for weeks

Then as I walk in the direction of the store
Every single time I head down the street
The mothers make me realize something important
Something special and normally ignored
The mother I already have is the one I wish to search for

My mother cuddles with me on a cold wet night
My mother bakes cookies with me on the weekend
My mother offers bandages and boo boo cures
My mother reads with me while lying in bed for sleep
Even if I asked for the same story for weeks

Even if there was a Mother Store
Even if I could go down there right now
I wouldn't pick another mother out of all the ones in stock
My mother is the perfect mother
There is no one better even when she yells

Throw It!

Cat Hartliebe

Throw it! Throw it! Throw it!
If only I could yell.
My tail wags excitedly
As Master waves it around.

Throw it! Throw it! Throw it!
I swear my bouncing
Makes it super obvious
I want the ball in the air.

Throw it! Throw it! Throw it!
Master needs to understand
I want the ball in my mouth.
Make it airborne, Master!

Throw it! Throw it! Throw it!
Master threw it! She really did!
Where is it? I lost it!
Master will never play with me again...

Throw it! Throw it! Throw it!
Master found the ball.
She looks ready to throw again
She'll play with me! Throw it!

Breathe in
Cat Hartliebe

Breathe in, breathe out.

The steady rhythm.

Keep the beat.

Breathe in, breathe out.

For everything.

Life needs it.

Breathe in, breathe out.

The machines beeps.

Try again quickly.

Breathe in, breathe out.

You need deeper.

Stop the machine.

Breathe in, breathe out.

Call for help.

Save the life.

Breathe in, ...

Beep, beep, beep.

Breaking Out
Beulah Pockets

Jodie was running
Running and running
Faster than the guards
They would catch her
She knew they would
They'd have to kill her
She'd die or she'd run
Either way she'd be out
Either way she'd be free
Shots rang out
Dogs barked
Men yelled
It didn't matter
There was the fence
She reached out her hand
Her fingers touched metal
The feeling went through her
A huge wave gripping
Making her stiff
She couldn't think
She knew it was over
They didn't reach her
Never made it in time
Now she is out
And they can't force her back

At the Aquarium
Cyro Hartliebe

Water surrounds me
In every direction
    Turtles
    Dolphins
    Octopuses

Workers start feeding
The very hungry
    Sharks
    Crocodiles
    Fish

I am amazed
By the awesome
    Otters
    Ducks
    Seals

Plant

Skyling De'Ambroise

Growing slowly
From the ground
Stems and leaves
Not a sound

Over time
You will see
A garden forms
For you and me

Mother's Wishes
Skyling De'Ambroise

You kid, you think

you know everything,

But take a moment and listen

to your mother's wishing.

She has been

where you are today.

So listen to her wishing;

she will lead the way.

Upon Return

Cat Hartliebe

The middle of the room

Surrounded by people

All the shouting and calling

I shiver and shake surprised

Where did they even come from?

I note slowly who is about me

Friends and family grin and cheer

A banner screams at me WELCOME

I am home; I made it back.

Others didn't and that has me saddened.

But really I must feel grateful I lived.

Run Away
Cat Hartliebe

My foot keeps hitting the ground.
It has to keep hitting the ground.
One foot than another
Since that which chases never slows down.

Foolishly I gaze back
To see things chasing me down.
Some are quite slow and docile.
Others make body builders run scared.

At rare and not so rare times,
I come to a sudden stop.
My heart can give up on me,
Or people could block the road.

Then the things that're chasing me
Catch up without any issue.
I'm floundering in the chaos,
The evil shadows of lost hope.

Thoughts and Feelings

Sun
Skyling De'Ambroise

Burning brightly
In the sky
Giving life
To plants nearby

Warmth and light
To all it brings
Let it shine
Upon your skin

Books
Cyro Hartliebe

No home is complete without a library.
A library offers books.
Books offer knowledge.
Books offer help.
Books offer hope.
No life is complete without books.

Electricity
Cyro Hartliebe

You can be shocking

You can be helpful

You can be fun to play with

You can make night safer

You can make work easier

You can make life brighter

Thank you

Sun
Cyro Hartliebe

Sun
Bright, hot
Burning, warming, flaring
Shining celestrial body
Star

Lost Childhood

Cat Hartliebe

After childhood flies away

Leaving your body old and haggard

Contemplating whether this grass is greener

It's hard to realize the simplicity

Of the childhood innocence and happiness

Sitting beneath the worn down tree

You used to climb when life was young

Where did that time go?

Seeking the Best Age

Cat Hartliebe

When you were born, you wanted to grow.

Everyone told you to grow up big and strong.

As you made it to three, you were too small to do.

So you wanted to grow up to real childhood.

At seven or eight, you begged to reach teenager.

The teens could do anything that you couldn't do.

By the time high school was around you,

College sounded way better; just need to be a few years older.

Skipping ahead, in college you sought being an adult.

A real job, a real house; not living at home.

By the time you had that child of your own,

You realized the best age was when you were born.

Rebirth by Fire
Cyro Hartliebe

Friday, the fire started.

A campfire flared.

The woods burns.

Nothing survived.

Sunday, the rain poured.

A new life formed.

The woods sprouted.

Everything regrew.

Shock and Awe
Cat Hartliebe

Before there were fireworks

The sky still made a show

During every thunder storm

People would certainly know

Nature offers the crack and streak

As lightning barrels by

As long as it doesn't hit

It creates beauty in the sky

The Months

Cat Hartliebe

Note:: Yes it is a sonnet.

The plants are poking up out of the ground.

Green sprouts will cover everything for now.

Then, pretty flowers grace the world around.

Before the seeds turn hard and start to bow.

In the middle of June or May, it's nice

To see an entire meadow filled by

Colorful blooms of a different price.

It leads to a very jealous July.

Not to mention the months before May day,

Who cannot make anyone stand still long.

March and February have less to say

Against the winter's charm or summer's song.

Each month has value, everyone should know,

Just some months are better at the big show.

Death is Sad
Cyro Hartliebe

Sickness is sad.

Failure is sad.

Absence is sad.

Losing is sad.

Memorials are sad.

Loss is sad.

Death is sad.

Debt is sad.

Theft is sad.

Collections are sad.

Missing is sad.

Funerals are sad.

Cemeteries are sad.

Death is sad.

Things I Love
Cyro Hartliebe

Cats
Grandma
Tomatos
Watching T.V.
Reading everywhere
Everything with ketchup
Tae Kwon Do with Master Woo
Green peas with mashed potatos
Being with my Uncle Dave all day
Pokemon Go in downtown Toms River

Things I love

Tomato
Cyro Hartliebe

Terrific
Oval
Marvelous
Awesome
Tasty
Outstanding

Stillness
Moe Destoryer

All things quiet

All things motionless

When all things stop

It is all it takes to be still

I Wish
Cyro Hartliebe

I wsh I could run away

From sadness to happiness

Sometimes sadness hurts

So I keep running to happiness

Food
Skyling De'Ambroise

Delightful tastes

Upon my tongue

Once it is eaten

Then it is done

Balloon
Moe Destoryer

Floating in the sky over the water

Blowing in the wind

Gliding like there's nowhere to be

Sliding on the wind for all to see

Running
Cyro Hartiebe

Running is fun.
I chase balls.
I chase flying leaves.
I chase frisbees.

Light
Cyro Hartliebe

Hopeful, abstract
Shining, glowing, warming
Opposite of dark
Brightness

Time
Cyro Hartliebe

Something that is always ticking.
Something that you never waste.
Something that I always waste.
Time is very valuable.

Hunger

Cyro Hartliebe

My hand grasped for the upper branches

Seeking out delicious leaves

But time of year denies me them

On bushes, there could be berries

My feet land softly on the ground

Running toward the bare branches

But no berries are to be found

On plants, bark is all that is left

Book
Moe Destoryer

Going into a land of unknown

Where you can be whatever you want

No matter what aspects you are

You can transform your environment

And perception for all to believe

You can do whatever you want

Inside a book

My Favorite Time
Cyro Hartliebe

Cloud-covered night sky

Echoing Brown Bats

Suspicious Eastern Raccoons

Missing loud traffic

Glowing bright fireflies

Loudly chirping crickets

My favorite time

Plant
Moe Destoryer

All things bloom with beautiful flowers

All things bloom with tasty treats

All things bloom with pretty leaves

All things are plants that bloom uncontrollably

Anger

Cyro Hartliebe

Teeth clench

Stance

Hands clench

Glare

Muscles clench

Punch

Myths and Legends

The Archer Readies
Cat Hartliebe

The archer readies

The shot comes

It will

Forever, he readies

Waiting

For an event coming

That never seems to come

The archer readied

Still readying

Caught by wood on four sides

Trapped by a curator

Keeping it safe

Safely readying

To shoot at an enemy

No longer present in our world

Ride with Ice
Cyro Hartliebe

As Ice and I took off,

Joy jumped inside me like ping pong balls.

The wind blew through my hair,

As we flew into the sunset.

As we landed on the ground,

My joy started to calm down.

The worst part was how quick the ride went.

The best part was touching the clouds.

How Clouds are Formed
Cyro Hartliebe

Unicorns gallop in the sky

Much like horses running by.

Every step they take,

Clouds formed in their wake.

Unicorns block the sun

Allowing for a lot more fun.

The clouds open up over me

Which ends our running spree.

Siren

Cat Hartliebe

Dancing on the edge
The cliff face down below
Water and rocks would capture me
Falling seems so silly

The harsh wind blew
I trip and miss the ground
Falling down to the ocean
My last breath above ground

Wakening is weird
Gills keep me alive
A song beats in my heart
Where am I?

The mood turns sour
I race for the noise
Men cajoling on a boat
I sing to make them realize

This is my life now
Drawn to noise and laughter
To sing brave sailors to their death
It brings joy to my forever after

Dragon Types
Cat Hartliebe

All the dragons in the world flying free
The colors grace the sky of starlight by
Coasting through the fluffy cloud and tall tree
Which colors will you spot on the fly by?

The korresurgics are the darker types
White, black, red, green and blue tossing you out
Crafting fear, dancing dreams, and showing swipes
These five dragons leave anyone devout.

Metalurgics complete the whole spectrum
They're the type to sparkle in the daylight
Silver, gold, bronze, copper, and electrum
Make me feel as if my time is tonight

If only the sky has such beasts flying,
Everyone would cower with such sighting.

Dinosaurs

Moe Destoryer

When they walked the earth, they were mighty.

When they walked the earth, they were majestic.

When they walked the earth, they were powerful.

Now that they don't walk the earth, they are honored.

Dinosaurs: Late Cretaceous

Cyro Hartliebe

T Rex on the ground.

Pterosaur in the air.

Iguanodon by the water.

I wish I was there.

Traveler

Cat Hartliebe

The jungle calls your name
The life is teeming there
The trees and snakes expect you
But do you actually care?

You will live where ever you wish
And see whatever you wish to see
Nothing stands in your way
Not sand, animals, or sea

The desert seemed boring
The ocean was quite dull
Back to the jungle you return
Into the tree house you call home

"Across the Universe"

Cat Hartliebe

Note:: NASA beamed a song - The Beatles' "Across the Universe" - directly into deep space at 7 p.m. EST on Feb. 4, 2008.

For thousands of years humans have roamed
But aliens would not see us
They would see giant monsters
The ones we call dinosaurs
Everywhere that is earth

The aliens look at our incoming items
And stare at our world thinking and wondering
What type of knowledge did those big guys make
Are they the pets or
Are they the ones speaking

For thousands of years humans have roamed
But aliens would not see us
We are new to earth
The dinosaurs would be even more terrifying
Singing "Across the Universe"

One Horned Wonder
Cat Hartliebe

Magestic beautiful perfect creatures
The world considers them legend and myth
Unicorns have the most well known features
Unicorns are as well known as Joe Smith

Much like a horse riding across the plains
Speed like an bullet or the fastest train
Just innocence will be all that remains
Unicorns are not known as inhumane

They're greatest piece of power is the horn
Sitting in the middle of the forehead
It's been that way since before we were born
"It's their mightiest weapon," many said

I cannot say for sure or fact what is
But unicorns sound dangerous no quiz

Majestic
Moe Destoryer

Imaginary and majestic
Mysterious and magnificent
Heavenly and pure
Unicorns are the ones to see
For the beauty they make us feel
For us to imagine what they are

Tiamat
Cyro Hartliebe

Sea animals are awesome
Every animal under the sea
Answers to the goddess Tiamat

Life surrounded by water
Is the world of Tiamat
For eternity and beyond
Enûma Elish explains everything.

Dragons

Skyling De'Ambroise

Teeths like swords

Scales like steel

Breath like death

Creates much fear

Tail like a whip

Wings like a bat

Eyes piercing thru you

Frightening to look at

Blue Dragon
Moe Destoryer

Majestically flying for all to see

The one who is as bright as the sea

Gliding right over the sea is the beauty

That is impossible to see

Blue dragon takes flight

So we all can believe that everything

Will be alright in the sea

The Truth
Cat Hartliebe

Green slimy scales covering towering terrors
Quick buglike things opening doors
Millions of minions capturing damsels
The impossible to defeat shadows of dark
Lizards the size of the Empire State Building
Or apes running wild through downtown

Nothing is as scary, not even these,
Of the rich white man staring you down

Beauty is in the Eye of the Beholder
Cat Hartliebe

'Beauty is in the eye of the beholder'.
This beholder doesn't quite understand.
If everyone sees beauty differently
Why then are there top rated looks?

'Beauty is in the eye of the beholder'.
My favorites are the opposite of the nation.
The prettiest ones are different or dark
And all I see is white static. Why?

'Beauty is in the eye of the beholder'.
My likes aren't acceptable supposedly.
My view is wrong; that makes no sense.
Why can't I say who I think is beautiful?

'Beauty is in the eye of the beholder'
Is a big fat ugly lie where I stand.
Beauty has a standard that makes no sense.
Topple the standard and make this quote truth.

ABOUT THE AUTHORS

Cat Hartliebe: Although she's managed a few poetry books in her life, she spends more of her time writing fantasy and fiction. You can easily see more of her work at any online book retailer.

Cyro Hartliebe: This is Cyro's second poetry book attempt. He works hard on Young Writer's Program (Nanowrimo's children off shoot) and finally has a complete first draft. Expect to see more of him in the world of writing sooner rather than later. He has a long life ahead of him.

Beulah Pockets: Yes, that is her real name. She's had many years writing. Most of those words written were not in poetry. But it was anything for Cyro.

Moe Destoryer: Moe isn't much of a writer. He loves to read and play games. This is his first poetry book attempt, hopefully, not his last.

Skyling De'Ambroise: A fantasy writer in normal senses, he hasn't managed to reach publishment stage. Often Skyling will recite poetry made up on the spot to his friends, family, and random passersby on the street.

44049204R00033